The
Source
of
Music

Sri Chinmoy

AUM PUBLICATIONS
NEW YORK

The Source of Music

Sri Chinmoy

ISBN 0-88497-575-4

Published by:
Aum Publications

CONTENTS

ONE

Music and Spirituality

If we can feel that
    It is not our voice,
    Not our fingers,
But some reality deep inside our heart
    Which is expressing itself,
Then we will know that it is
    The soul's music.

The outer music
Comes from an outer instrument.
   The inner music
Comes from the heart.
The name of this inner music
   Is oneness.

*M*usic is the inner or universal language of God. I do not know French or German or Italian. But if music is played, immediately the heart of the music enters into my heart, or my heart enters into the music. At that time, we do not need outer communication; the inner communion of the heart is enough. My heart is communing with the heart of the music and in our communion we become inseparably one.

In the spiritual world, next to meditation is music, the breath of music. Meditation is silence, energising and fulfilling. Silence is the eloquent expression of the inexpressible. Aldous Huxley says: "After silence, that which comes nearest to expressing the inexpressible is music."

Silence is the source of everything. It is the source of music and it is music itself. Silence is the deepest, most satisfying music of the Supreme. Silence is like a stream that goes to one place and becomes a river, or to another place and becomes a brook, or to the sea, where it is totally expanded.

Silence is the nest and music is the bird. The bird leaves the nest early in the morning and returns to the nest in the evening. Similarly, in the spiritual world, divine music comes from the inmost soul of silence.

Soulful Music

Soulful music immediately awakens and inspires our hearts because it embodies the Absolute Supreme. Soulful music is the Light that wants to express itself in a divine way. Even as darkness wants to manifest its authority on earth, Light also wants to manifest its Reality and Divinity in a specific way. Light is the soul of everything. Light is the soul of music, Light is the soul of love and Light is the soul of all art. When Light divinely manifests itself in the form of music, it is the music of the soul.

Music means Self-expansion and oneness. The Self expands through music. The Self that expands is not the individual self but the unlimited Self. Music is the expansion of unlimited Reality.

We can use music to help us in our spiritual life provided we know that music and the spiritual life are like twin brothers; we cannot separate them. How can we separate two fingers, two eyes? They sit side by side. If one eye is not functioning well, then we feel that our vision is imperfect. Similarly, music and the spiritual life must go together; one complements the other. Music helps the spiritual seeker to go deep within to get the utmost satisfaction from life, from truth, from reality. The spiritual life, in turn, helps music to offer its capacity and its strength, which is the soul's light, to the world at large.

When we listen to soulful music, or when we ourselves play soulful music, immediately our inner existence climbs up high, higher, highest. It climbs up and enters into something beyond. This Beyond is constantly trying to help us, guide us, mould us and shape us into our true transcendental image, our true divinity. When we hear soulful music, or when we play a soulful piece of music, we feel a kind of inner thrill in our entire existence, from the soles of our feet to the crown of our head. A river is flowing through us, a river of consciousness, and this consciousness is all the time illumined.

Music and Meditation

Next to deep prayer or meditation, music is of paramount importance. Meditation is like a direct route, or shortcut, to the goal. Music is a road that is absolutely clear: it may be a little longer, but it is quite clear of obstacles. If we can play soulful music or hear soulful music, the power of our meditation increases. Soulful music adds to our aspiration. Similarly, if a spiritual seeker wants to be a musician, even if he does not have a musical background, he will be able to be a good musician because prayer and meditation contain all capacities. You may never have studied music, but if you pray and meditate soulfully, then inside your prayer, inside your meditation, by the Grace of the Supreme, the power of music looms large. Then you can utilise this power in your own way.

Each time soulful music is played, we get inspiration and delight. In the twinkling of an eye, music can elevate our consciousness. But if we also pray and meditate, then we are undoubtedly more illumined and fulfilled than a music-lover who is not consciously leading a spiritual life. Each spiritual musician is consciously spreading God's Light on earth. God is the cosmic Player, the eternal Player, and we are His instruments. It is the Supreme who makes the proper instrument. Then, it is He who makes the player play properly, and it is He who makes the musician.

The Power of Music

Soulful and spiritual music really helps us; it feeds our inner life. Music has tremendous power. With fire we can burn ourselves, or we can cook and do many other good things. It is the same with music. Divine music immediately elevates our consciousness, whereas undivine music immediately lowers our consciousness and tries to destroy our sincere inner cry for a better spiritual life. The spiritual person will immediately be affected by this music. So music can change our consciousness provided it is the music that comes from the heart and enters into the heart. The music that touches the very depth of our heart can elevate our consciousness.

The Mind and the Senses

Our senses are restless. Therefore, our mind suffers. Our mind is doubtful. Therefore, our senses suffer. The mind has no capacity to bind or discipline the senses. Here music comes to the mind's rescue. With the help of music, the mind binds and disciplines the senses and makes them into perfect instruments so they can be inundated with peace, light and bliss from above.

Again, when the mind is doubtful, when the mind drinks deep of doubt-poison, the senses have no capacity to inject faith into the mind. Here also music comes to the rescue. The senses take help from music to transform and illumine themselves. When the senses are calm and quiet, the doubtful mind is totally transformed and it becomes inseparably one with the heart, which is all receptivity. At that time our Inner Pilot—the Supreme Musician—can manifest Himself blessingfully, powerfully and measurelessly. As He is manifesting Himself in and through us, the divine music becomes part and parcel of our existence and we grow into perfect Perfection. In and through us the Supreme Musician creates a new world. We become the divine music, and a new vision of God's transcendental Reality operates in and through us.

Can spiritual music be played during meditation?

Certainly, although it depends on the one who meditates. There are many seekers on earth who meditate extremely well, but who have not developed their musical sense. Their ears have not been trained, so we cannot expect them to change their nature overnight. They either lack the capacity of appreciation or they have some austere feeling about music. Psychic music is not very widely appreciated, and very few people appreciate the soul's music. They feel it is like a stranger that is entering into their consciousness. But it is actually their eternal tenant, their soul, that is deep within them waiting to come to the fore.

If divine music is played during deep meditation, it enhances the meditation. It will immediately help in elevating the consciousness. If you are fond of music, then playing soulful songs or chants during your meditations at home will definitely help you.

Were we to play spiritual music on tape while we slept, would it benefit us in any way?

While you are sleeping if you play soulful music, your subtle vital, subtle physical and subtle mind will enjoy it. But your physical body may find it difficult to appreciate it, for it wants total silence. Although soulful music will add to pure silence, inner silence, the physical body wants a kind of silence which is totally devoid of outer sound.

If you play your tape very softly, it will definitely help and inspire the subtle physical and subtle vital which are not sleeping.

Many, many times when the physical sleeps, the subtle physical and the subtle vital do not sleep. They move around. They roam here and there. They visit their friends and enemies. My music is definitely a source of joy to them. So for the subtle physical, subtle vital and subtle mind, undoubtedly it is a help. But for the gross physical which is trying to sleep, it may be a hindrance, a disaster.

What is the supreme duty of an artist or musician?

The supreme duty of an artist or musician is to meditate before he creates something and, while creating, to be in a very contemplative, divine mood. Then, when the creation is completed, he will immediately offer his creation to the Supreme. No matter what others say about his creation, no matter what his feelings are about his own creation, as soon as his creation is completed, he will offer it to the Supreme for Him to use in His own way. This is the supreme duty of the spiritual musician or artist.

Is creativity another form of meditation?

It depends on what you are creating. If it is spiritual art or music, then certainly it is a form of meditation. But if you play undivine music or write unbearable books or keep your mind in the gutter while you are painting, this is not any kind of meditation. While you are creating, if your consciousness is in the lower vital world, it will not be a form of meditation. But if you are singing something soulful or if you are in a very high consciousness while you are creating, if you are giving yourself in a divine way to the object or subject that you are involved with, then definitely you are doing a form of meditation. You have to know what you are creating and where your consciousness is while you are doing it.

I am giving a lot of importance to aspiring through music.

There is nothing wrong if you feel aspiration in your music. But you have to know how many hours you can think of your music. If you spend five hours, six hours, seven hours a day on music, then you should spend one hour or two hours, let us say, on spirituality. Music is also a form of spirituality; I do not deny it. But the height that you will achieve from meditation either you may not get or cannot get from your music. Music is an added help.

10

If you can play spiritual music, soulful music, then you will have no problem in your life. But if you play only mundane music, then you may not be satisfied. You may be pleasing the outer world, but you are not pleasing your Inner Pilot in His own way. If you are not an aspiring seeker, that is fine. But if you are a sincere seeker, then you will feel miserable.

When I play music, I feel a tingling around my third eye.

That indicates an awakening. But this does not mean that your third eye is about to open. No. When you play most soulfully, an inner vision-light will come to the fore. Vision is within you, yet it is dormant. But now it wants to function properly; it does not want to sleep anymore. So inner vision is starting to operate. The vision of the third eye is trying to come to the fore, and that is why you are getting that sensation. It is a very good experience.

What is the soundless sound, and can it serve as a bridge between the manifest and the unmanifest worlds?

As it stands now the outer world is not at all aware of the inner world. So first the outer world has to be fully aware of the inner world, and then it has to listen to the blessingful dictates of the inner world. Then the soundless sound—which is now heard only by very, very few Truth-seekers and God-lovers—can be of divine service to mankind. It is an inner discovery. This discovery has to be brought to the fore, and for that the outer world has to be consciously awakened and devotedly accept the beauty and divinity of the inner world.

The soundless sound is something real, absolutely real. But we hear it only in our highest realm of consciousness, or when we dive deep within and reach the inmost recesses of our heart. The soundless sound is infinitely, infinitely more powerful than any man-made sound. But up to now, it has been operating only in the inner world. So those who have a free access to the inner world can hear this sound. Not only do they derive tangible benefit from this sound, but it helps the seekers and God-lovers immensely in their self-giving life to God the Creator and God the creation.

O music of love,
From you I learn
The secret of closeness.

O music of silence,
From you I learn
The secret of universal oneness.

How many songs have I sung?
How many more have I still to sing
    Here on earth?
Within and without
I have been searching for myself
    Through my songs.
With deep pangs my heart cries;
My Self-Form is not visible yet.
In the vast life-ocean,
I am floating all alone.

You are nothing but beauty, eternal beauty,
Wherever I turn my eyes.
Do You always drink the nectar
Of Your Self-Form
Residing in my eyes?
The waves of tune
And sweet and melodious songs
That create heart-elevating resonance,
O Beloved, do You hear them
By using my ears?

TWO

Vital Music and Illumination-Music

Human music
Feeds the vital of mankind.
Divine music
Serves the heart of mankind.

A seeker-singer feels that if he has no music, his heart is soulless, his life is useless, his goal is worthless.

Why? Because music is the oneness-aspiration of humanity. Oneness without a soulful melody is blind, deaf and useless.

Again, a melody without fruitful oneness is just a body without a soul.

Without oneness-aspiration, humanity can never achieve perfection.

Without perfection, satisfaction will always remain a far cry.

If there is no satisfaction, then life can have no value whatsoever.

It is for satisfaction that we aspire. It is for satisfaction that we try to perfect ourselves.

Satisfaction is the only reality-existence that both God and man need.

Soulful music not only has the answer, but is the answer to this need.

The seven notes in the scale correspond to the seven higher worlds. Each note comes down from a specific inner world. Each world has a music of its own and a note of its own. The higher worlds have a music that awakens us, inspires us, illumines us, perfects us and fulfils us. The music of the higher worlds constantly comes to us as the harbinger of the highest Height, whereas the music of the lower worlds naturally comes to us as a messenger of destruction.

It is not only the higher and lower worlds that have a music of their own; each individual has his own music, each movement has its own music, each action has its own music. Each time we breathe in and breathe out, there is music. When we do not pay attention to the inner depth of the action, we do not hear the music. If we do pay adequate attention to each action, then inside the very depth of that action we are bound to hear music. Unless we hear music inside each action, the action is lifeless.

Next to meditation is music. But it has to be soulful music, the music that stirs and elevates our aspiring consciousness. When we play soulful music, psychic music, then immediately we are transported to the highest realm of consciousness.

This music from the soul wants to express and fulfil itself through the heart. But here a problem arises. When the soul starts to play its music in the heart, the doubting mind does not allow the heart to listen. Then gradually the vital* becomes more powerful than the pure heart.

The music of the lower vital destroys our subtle nerves and wants to devour the heart's divine qualities. The vital has been predominant in the world for quite a few years. But lower vital music will not always predominate on earth. The world also has a soul. Eventually, the music of the soul will replace the music of the vital. Today the vital is nourished and the soul is starving. But when there are more aspiring people than unaspiring people on earth, naturally the inner, soul-elevating music will replace the music of the impure, unlit and obscure vital.

When we play vital music, we starve our soul and feed our body. The creator is like the mother and humanity is the child. When the creator plays vital music, the mother is drinking something, but the child is starving for something else, for milk. But

---

*The vital is the web of desires, motives, drives and emotions. It can include—in its higher and illumined aspect—aspiration, or the quest for illumination and perfection. But unless the term 'higher vital' or 'illumined vital' is used, the vital usually refers to worldly desires and the quest for possessions and power. [Ed.]

when the creator plays spiritual music, both the mother and the child are drinking nectar at the same time. Even looking at the mother's face, the child will be able to drink nectar. The very fact that the mother is drinking nectar is enough for the child.

The Soul's Light and Delight

Soulful music offers delight rather than vital excitement. Vital excitement is one thing and the soul's delight is something else. The soul's delight is most powerful, most intense but, at the same time, it does not create any kind of undivine, sensational pleasure in the body. It just transports; it carries the entire being into the Highest like a balloon and then, when the balloon breaks, you are swimming in the sea of bliss.

Soulful music is the music that immediately elevates our consciousness to the Absolute, to the Highest. But ordinary music, vital music, may bring our consciousness down. For a fleeting second or a few hours, we get a kind of pleasure; but then this pleasure takes us into a lower vital consciousness. Soulful music takes us into the world of aspiration. From aspiration we enter into the world of realisation, where our inner existence is flooded with light and delight.

The Universal Consciousness

Soulful music is the music that wants to eventually transform our consciousness. It carries us into the Universal Consciousness and makes us feel that we are in tune with the highest, with the deepest, with the farthest. It also makes us feel that God Himself is the Supreme Musician.

A soulful sound gives immediate joy and immediate self-expansion. This self-expansion is not egocentric; it is something divine, something supreme, something universal. A soulful sound is like music that is produced for all. With it the 'I' goes away. In soulful sound there is no 'I'. It is all 'we'. Other sounds are produced by the individual for the individual, but a soulful sound is produced by the Universal in us, by the Eternal in us, by the Absolute in us. The soulful sound is of Eternity and for Infinity and Immortality. This is how we distinguish the soulful sound from other sounds. Other sounds have their originality in individuality, but soulful sounds have their originality in universality.

The Divine Musician

The human musician plays in order to become great. The divine musician becomes good first and then plays divinely, while soulfully and unconditionally offering the results to his Beloved Supreme.

You have to know that if you play music from the vital plane, you are only fooling yourself. The music that is inspired from around or below the navel is the vital music. Music that comes from the heart is psychic music, and the music that comes from the inmost recesses of the heart, from very deep within, comes from the soul. If we can feel that it is not our voice, not our fingers, but some reality deep inside our heart which is expressing itself, then we will know that it is the soul's music.

When we play soulful music, we elevate our consciousness most rapidly. Soulful music is a form of aspiration, a form of meditation. All those who are seekers of the infinite Truth will naturally play soulful music; and when they play soulful music, they have to know that they are consciously running towards their destined goal.

Music and Consciousness

Water symbolises consciousness. Consciousness, like water, is neutral. What we put inside water is of paramount importance. If it is something harmless, sweet and divine, then we will get joy. But if we put something undivine, poisonous and destructive in the water, then naturally when we drink it we shall die. What we mix with the water before drinking it is entirely up to us. When you hear music, if it lifts your consciousness, then you will know that it is spiritual music. Sometimes the musician is aspiring and also he is playing spiritual music; at that time you are very fortunate, because you get both.

Musicians should give something new; they should give the world music that comes directly from the soul, music that will help humanity raise its consciousness—not the things that have been known for many, many years, but the things that people have never seen or felt or heard.

Vital music played its role, especially in the Western hemisphere. But this kind of music is not the soul's music. The soul's music is something totally different. The world will eventually appreciate, admire and adore that music.

Music is of God and for God, not of the vital world and for the vital world. Real music, divine music, takes you back to God, the Supreme Musician.

Can listening to music raise one's consciousness?

If you listen to and identify yourself with spiritual music, music from the heart and soul, naturally it will raise your consciousness. But if you listen to ordinary vital music, then it will lower your consciousness.

Soulful music already has its own height. While you are listening, you identify with it, so like a magnet it pulls you up. Already the height is there.

If somebody has already gone to the top floor of a building, it means that there is a staircase. You have to identify yourself with the staircase and also with the person who has already climbed up it. Then only will he be able to show you how he climbed up and where the staircase is. Appreciation means identification. If you become one with the staircase and also with the person who has created the staircase for you in his music, then you also can reach the top floor.

In years to come, what songs will have the greatest influence on humanity?

The songs that will have the greatest influence are those that come directly from the soul and immediately are accepted by the aspiring heart, vital, mind and body. Sometimes you can soulfully sing most soulful songs, but only the aspiring heart accepts the songs. The doubting mind or the intellectual mind finds it very difficult to appreciate anything. The aggressive or restless vital and the sombre or sleeping body also find it very difficult to appreciate the songs. But when a soulful song is sung soulfully and, at the same time, it is appreciated by the immediate members of the inner family–the body, vital, mind and heart–on the soul level on which it is sung, then it will definitely have the greatest influence on humanity.

Sometimes you sing a song most soulfully from the heart level, let us say. If it is not appreciated on the heart level, if it is just appreciated on the mind level or the vital level or the physical level, then one does not get the utmost joy, inspiration and satisfaction from it. In order to get the utmost satisfaction, one has to reach the level from which the song is sung and appreciate it there before it comes down to a lower level. If it is from the heart level, then one has to attain the heart level in order to appreciate it. One can also appreciate it from a lower rung, but it will not be as effective.

In your books you say that vital music can be detrimental to our spiritual life. But sometimes when I listen to music that is very lively and up tempo, I feel I get joy. It is not what you would call spiritual music; it is just energetic music. Do you consider this kind of energetic music detrimental?

There are two aspects of the vital. There is the dynamic vital and the tempting and tempted vital. When Sri Chaitanya and his disciples used to sing and dance in the street, they were not manifesting the tempting or tempted vital. No, it was the dynamic vital, which is full of enthusiasm to scatter its dynamic energy all around. The vital that is energised in a pure way—the vital that is trying to elevate the consciousness of those around it—is absolutely necessary. This kind of eagerness, enthusiasm and dynamism is very good.

But there is another kind of vital that also has dynamic energy but that brings the consciousness low, lower, lowest. Easily your mind and your heart can see the difference. I do not want to use the terms 'rock and roll' or 'jazz'. What do I know about those things? But if you want to make a comparison between music that comes from the dynamic vital and music that comes from the tempting or tempted vital, easily you can see the difference. From this other kind of music, you may get enthusiasm, but it is not the pure enthusiasm that will elevate your consciousness or spiritual life. While you are in that world of music, you will notice your consciousness going down, or you will find that it has gone down.

Sometimes we are not aware when our consciousness is being lowered. It is only when our consciousness has reached the abysmal abyss that we see what has happened. While we are climbing a little way down the tree, we think, "This is nothing, nothing! I can easily climb back up." But we cannot. Once we start to descend, we continue to descend. We cannot stay in one place; the law of gravity takes over and we fall to the bottom.

So you have to see what kind of vital energy the music has—whether it is taking you upward or bringing you downward. You have to be the judge.

In today's world, it seems increasingly difficult for artists and musicians to survive. Is there any advice you have for the multitude of struggling artists? And what is it that determines the difference between whether they are truly successful or not?

I am a Truth-seeker and God-lover. In my case, if a musician or an artist can waken the consciousness of the audience to a higher height, then I feel that he is successful; he has made a tremendous contribution to the world at large. But again there are some musicians—and in no way am I criticising them; that is what they like and also what the audience likes—who create a kind of excitement in the vital region. Then it does not go any farther. It only touches the exciting vital and stimulates the vital, and it all ends in eventual frustration. Whereas if some musicians play soulful music and some singers sing soulfully, they are bound to awaken the consciousness of the audience. After all, each individual who comes to listen to songs or to hear music comes to get something abiding—the lasting joy that inspires them to see and feel something in themselves that is absolutely new and unprecedented—unprecedented joy, unprecedented love.

The present-day musicians are the musicians who play vital music. They create lightning excitement for the music-lovers. But excitement is not the answer to humanity's evolution. It is the soulful awakening that is of paramount importance. Soulful music awakens the heart; the soul is already awakened. The soul is always awakened, but the soul tries to manifest God's Beauty, Light and Power in and through the body, vital, mind and heart.

So it depends on the individual musician. If he wants to awaken the consciousness of his listeners and give them something divine and immortal, then he has to enter into their aspiring lives on the strength of his own aspiration—which is his offering through his musical talents.

Each type of music has access to a particular realm. Vital music cannot be used as a vehicle for spiritual growth—it is like knocking on the wrong door. When musicians play vital music, I do not think they are meditating on the soul. They are aiming at excitement and noise, and a kind of, I do not want to say 'confusion', but a kind of destruction. If you play soulful music, then you have to enter into the soulfulness of the music and also enter into the soulfulness of the audience. If my goal is situated in the north, then I will only get whatever is in the north; I will not get what is in the south.

Sincere God-lovers will not be satisfied when they hear music that is all excitement and vital exuberance. They will be satisfied only when there is something very soulful, very pure, very haunting, so that at every moment they feel they are entering into a higher realm of consciousness. This higher realm of consciousness is their goal, whereas other musicians who are playing vital music are not thinking of the goal as the highest or the greatest need in their life, nor does the audience think of that highest goal.

At my job I have to work with unspiritual music. How can I be creative and not be affected by it?

The best thing you can do is try not to be affected by the unspiritual music and remain in a high consciousness. Your best creation is not to be affected by something which is trying to lower your consciousness. Your creation is to maintain your spiritual height. If you can remain in your aspiration, that aspiration itself is creation.

I have been earning my living through music for about ten years, but now it is very difficult for me to take money for my art. I feel that I only want to serve God through music.

You have to know that money can either be a divine power, or it can be misused. With a knife we can cut a fruit and share it with our brothers and sisters, or we can stab others. Money as such is not bad, only we have to know how we are getting it and using it. We shall not get money by using foul means, and we shall not misuse money: this should be our attitude. Why should it be difficult for you to accept money for your music? Money can be God's blessing if you use it properly.

You have to know how you are earning your money. If you are singing lower vital, emotional songs and creating excitement, and if you feel that that is the only way you can earn money, it is absurd. You have to maintain your own standard. You will do something that will elevate the consciousness of others, not stimulate excitement. Vital music stimulates, whereas the soul's music, psychic music, elevates.

If you earn money by illumining and elevating somebody's consciousness and with that money you support yourself or do something good and divine, then how can anybody blame you? But you have to know how you are getting the money, from whom you are getting it and how you are using it. If you take all these things into consideration, then money-power need not be a stumbling block. Money-power is also God's power, but it has to be used properly.

THREE

Becoming an Instrument:
Composing and Performing

If you have haunting music
   In your mind
And a soulful song
   In your heart,
Then easily you will be able
To reveal an unknown world of beauty
   For the God-lovers.

I sing because You sing.
I smile because You smile.
Because You play on the flute,
I have become Your flute.
You play in the depths of my heart.
You are mine, I am Yours:
This is my sole identification.
In one Form You are
My Mother and Father eternal,
And Consciousness-moon,
Consciousness-sun all pervading.

*W*hen we play soulful music, we come to realise that we are not the musician; we are just an instrument. We are like a piano, violin or guitar, and it is God who is constantly playing on us. If we really play soulful music, we will see that we are just an instrument, that somebody else is singing and playing in and through us, and that somebody is our Inner Pilot, the Supreme.

The earthly creator we misunderstand because of his shortcomings. But he is bringing down his creation from another world, especially if he is a soulful musician. He brings down reality from a higher world on the strength of his intense aspiration, and for half an hour or an hour he remains high, very high. The music he writes or plays at that time comes from that high realm. But after half an hour or an hour he may enter into his ordinary consciousness again. That is why people appreciate a soulful musician while they listen to his music and later look down upon him for his human failings. Everything he has brought down from the very high worlds to illumine and fulfil the earth-consciousness is undoubtedly the representative and the reality of the life-breath of God coming down from the higher worlds.

Music is of God and for God. Real music, divine music, takes you back to God, the Supreme Musician. Divine music is of the heart and for the heart. If it is for the vital world, then those who play will have to live in that world. But if you want to live all the time in the soul's world, your music has to be totally different. Give the world the reality that you live. Even if the world does not appreciate it right now, still you have to remain faithful to your reality. If you are not playing the music that you live, the music that you are, then you will feel sorry. It is like living a double life. Your outer life must add to your inner life. Anything you do in the outer life has to be a proper expression of your inner life. If there is a yawning gulf between your inner life and your outer life, then you can never be happy.

If you are crying to see God's Light in your consciousness, then you have to give the world what you really are. If you bring to the fore music from the soul, then only will your contribution to humanity be significant. When artistic capacity is joined with spiritual capacity, the musician can break through the walls that other musicians have created. At that time, outer success will not only be worldly success but also divine success.

You may say that in the outer world you have to play undivine music. But you are in no way compelled! Just to attract the attention of the world, please do not let your spiritual life suffer. Sincerely follow the spiritual life. Try to bring the soul's music to the fore.

Can a work of art manifest a higher state of consciousness than the artist himself has actually attained?

An artist, just like an elevator, can go very high for a fleeting second and create something very high. Then, the next moment he can drop. But even if he falls as a human being, the thing that he has achieved remains at its original height. Perhaps the artist will never reach that same height in this incarnation again, but his artistic creation remains. But without reaching a certain height at least for a fleeting second, the artist cannot create anything at that particular height.

How can I overcome fear when I am performing in front of an audience?

When you play music, feel that it is not you who is playing. Somebody else is playing and somebody else is enjoying. But that somebody else is part of you.

One part of you is playing, one part is enjoying and still another part has become the music itself. So the moment you start playing, make yourself into three parts. Feel that one existence of yours is playing, another portion is observing and a third part of you is the music itself. You are the creator, you are the creation and you are the reality that exists in the creator and the creation. These things need not come as mental thoughts or images; far from it. At a glance they can come.

Sometimes when you play, on the strength of your heart's oneness with the audience, you can observe one thing. There are two hearts: one heart is your small heart, which is playing, and the other heart is the big heart, which is listening. Again, the big heart is playing and the small heart is listening. The audience is the larger heart and you are the smaller heart that is expanding and becoming one with the larger heart. When you are playing, try to feel this. And then feel that you are the larger heart and the audience is the smaller heart. If you have this experience, then you will feel that you were one and now you have become many, and that you were many and now you have become one.

This is what happens when the smaller heart and the larger heart meet together. The smaller heart is the seed and the larger heart is the tree. The seed grows into the tree and the tree gives birth to new seeds. If you can see it in this way, then at every moment your music will give the greatest satisfaction, for this moment you are the seed, the next moment you are the fruit. You are the fruit, you are the seed; you are the dream, you are the reality. This is what the heart feels.

Whenever you perform, feel that you are not performing in front of fifty people. Feel that there is only one person listening to you, and imagine that that person is a child only two years old. This is the human way.

The divine way is to see immediately the Supreme before you. If you see the Supreme and feel that you also are the Supreme, then how can one Supreme be afraid of the other Supreme? There is only one Supreme. If you bow down to the Supreme inside each individual in the audience, then immediately you become one with each individual. Then you will not be afraid. Because you do not feel your oneness, you are afraid. But if you are one, then you do not feel afraid. This is the divine way.

How can a person manifest the highest, most joyful music in his soul while playing a musical instrument?

While playing a musical instrument, you have to feel that music is the universal language, that music has and also is the key to unlock the Heart-Door of the Supreme. It is only music that has a free access to unlock the Heart-Door of the universal Heart of the Supreme. If you can do that, then the musician in you will be able to manifest the Highest.

When you meditate soulfully, early in the morning, you enter into a higher world, the world of divine reality, perfection and satisfaction. You can try to bring this world down into your music in a practical way. While you are breathing in and breathing out, try to feel that you are offering your life-breath to the instrument that you will use. Your life-breath is something very precious. Feel that you are offering your life's most precious possession to your instrument.

When the Supreme created you, He gave you a portion of His Reality, His Divinity. That was the supreme sacrifice. He gave something of Himself and created you. Try to feel that now you are creating something for the world. You are giving to your instrument something of yourself—something really precious and luminous, something which is part and parcel of your own reality. You are the instrument of the Supreme. He is using you, and you are using something else, your own instrument. It takes only a few seconds. You do not have to do this with all the strings. Just cast a glance at one or two and feel your life-breath inside. At that time, offer your gratitude to the Supreme, who gave you life itself, and feel that a portion of your life you are giving to your instrument. The Creator created you by offering you a portion of His Reality. Now He is asking you to create something in the same way.

Can we use meditation to increase our creativity?

Certainly! Prayer and meditation are the only way. Many people are not born poets or artists. But by practising meditation, they bring into their system literary capacities, painting capacities, musical capacities, because meditation means new life. When new life enters into you, you become a new person. Before you were not an artist, let us say. God gave you a particular type of life, with particular capacities. But when a new life enters into you, that means a new opportunity, a new avenue, a new light enters. At that time you can easily acquire creativity.

How can I make my music full of supreme beauty?

You can make your music full of supreme beauty if you can remember constantly that your music is only an extension of your inner consciousness and that it is also an expression of the divine within that is crying for manifestation. If you can accept or feel or be aware of the divine within you, then you can bring to your music, through the expression of your life's reality, the supreme beauty. But always feel that the divine within you has accepted music as an expression of its reality for your own perfection in life.

When you play music, you have to feel you are playing not to satisfy your vital, not to compete with others, not for the applause of the audience and not for name and fame. You have to feel that you are the instrument and the Supreme is playing in and through you. You are His instrument and He is playing you. He is the musician and, at the same time, He Himself is the listener. You have to feel that He is the player, He is the listener, and He is the instrument itself. If you have that kind of feeling, automatically divine perfection dawns in your music.

Does it make a difference if you play music from memory rather than reading it off a sheet of music?

If you are interested in the spontaneous fountain of the heart, it is better to play music by heart. Then you can give life to the music. When you read music, the eyes are seeing the paper and the mind is operating. At that time, the mental consciousness enters into the picture; the paper consciousness enters into the mind, and the spontaneous, soulful qualities are all gone. So let the fountain flow only from the heart. If you have another small fountain in the mind, in spite of having a big fountain in the heart, you are going to create a problem. Again, if you know all the notes but just play mechanically, that also is not good. You should learn the music by heart, but you should also give life to the music while playing. Reading music takes away from the spiritual quality, even though it is the usual method.

When someone feels a beautiful poem or song inside, what prevents its outer expression?

There are two main reasons. The first reason is that when you feel a poem or song, you doubt it; you doubt whether it is real or not. You feel, "Oh, how can I have that kind of beautiful feeling? Five minutes ago I told a lie, ten minutes ago I was jealous of somebody, so it is impossible to feel this way now." But what happened five minutes ago has nothing to do with what you are feeling right now.

The mind is so clever. When you have a wonderful experience, a very good, high experience, your mind will immediately try to throw cold water on it, because your mind does not want you to have joy in its pure form. Your mind will immediately ask you how you can experience this kind of thing when you acted so undivinely just a little while ago. The mind will say it is all mental hallucination. And the moment you give up the experience, the same mind will come and say, "See, you are such a fool! You have lost everything; you have thrown away everything. God alone knows how many months it will take you to get this experience back again."

The second reason why you cannot express a poem or song that you have inside you is that there is a gap between your feeling and your becoming. When you feel something, if you do not immediately become that thing, then your vital being revolts. The vital being feels that you have allowed a stranger to enter into you, and it becomes jealous. It acts just like a child when he sees that his mother and father have allowed somebody else to come and stay at his house. Naturally he becomes jealous because he feels that now his parents will not be able to pay as much attention to him as before. When you feel something inside you, it means that you have invited someone or something into your house, but he has not yet entered. Once he enters, the expression is as good as achieved, but before he enters the child may revolt. He may start crying and say, "I do not want him; I do not want him." But if the parents become serious and say, "We have invited him and he will definitely stay," then it is all over. Once you become what you feel, the difficulty is over.

These are the two main things that keep you from manifesting in your outer life what you feel within yourself.

How can I keep my ego out of my art?

You have to be clever. If the ego comes, then think that you are one individual and your ego is another. This other individual is undivine, but you are mixing with him. You have got a piece of bread and you are sharing it with somebody whom outwardly you call a friend. But from your personal inner experience you know that this ego is really your enemy. Why should you share with somebody who does not have the same goal as you have? The ego will stand in your way when you try to run toward your goal. By feeding someone who has a different goal from you, you are only delaying your own progress and weakening your own strength.

The Supreme is waiting for you; He is crying, crying for you to reach Him. Yet you are giving half your strength to somebody who is really your enemy. The Supreme gives you the opportunity and the capacity to run the fastest, but you are sharing half your capacity with somebody who is running to another goal, the goal of destruction. You have to feel at that time that he is a real enemy. If you see the ego in this way, then you can easily separate your creative capacity from your ego.

What kind of mental attitude should one have in learning to play music?

There is mental music, vital music and physical music. Again, there is something called soulful music. If one wants to get true delight from the heart and from the aspiring life, then he must dedicate his music to God. He must play soulful music—music that will inspire his own life of aspiration and inspire others who hear his music—not music that will excite his vital and arouse the physical consciousness.

Is spiritual music the music that makes you think more about God?

Let us say, more about satisfaction, light and delight. There may be great musicians who do not believe in God, but they do believe in satisfaction, joy and delight. If you play divine music, spiritual music, then you are bound to give and get satisfaction.

How can I retain my aspiration to manifest and serve God through my music and not be affected by the people involved in the music business who are concerned only with dollar signs?

You can transform the nature of those who care more for money than for real music. How? You have to make yourself feel at every moment that your music is not something to excite humanity but something to illumine humanity. If it is excitement, then only the vital is fed. If it is illumination, then the entire being is fed. When you think of music, always think of illumination. Take music as something that constantly illumines and not as something that brings money and will make you a multi-millionaire. Always make those people who are money-minded feel that it is illumination that can come from your music and not money-power.

Music can do much for the Supreme. It is a way to reach humanity and bring spirituality to humanity. The shopkeeper gives something to the customer and the customer appreciates it. Then, when the customer begins to have faith in that particular shopkeeper, the shopkeeper says, "You have appreciated my mango, but now I have something else for you; I have a guava also. This will also satisfy you and nourish you." Because the customer has faith in the shopkeeper, he will taste the new fruit and be satisfied. The time has come for musical people to say, "We can give you something else. It is called spirituality. Try it."

When a musician leads a spiritual life, it is very easy for him to help thousands of people at a time, because they appreciate his music and the kind of life he leads. Spiritual Masters can only approach humanity if people come to them with real aspiration, whereas musicians have the means to approach humanity with their art.

How can I bring spirituality into my music?

Each seeker-musician has a golden opportunity to please the Supreme with his music. Whenever you play music, you have to know whether or not that music is going to please the Supreme. If it pleases you and you feel it will please God, then play it. If you feel it will not please God, then never play it. Playing lower vital music to get appreciation from the public can never please the Supreme. If an ordinary person who has not launched into the spiritual life plays that kind of music, he is doing the right thing according to his own standard. But if a seeker plays that kind of music, he cannot make any progress.

A sincere seeker who has already accepted a path of his own should play only spiritual music, psychic music, music that elevates his consciousness and the consciousness of others. Play music that inspires you, that comes from the very depth of your heart and illumines your consciousness. When you play this kind of music, you will see that in each note God Himself is blossoming like a lotus, petal by petal. When you play divine music, please feel that God is unveiling His own inner Music and fulfilling Himself in and through you.

I am a musician and I am also trying to follow the spiritual life. I find it difficult to reconcile these two parts of myself, and I feel I shouldn't try to move too quickly in this area.

You may say that it is necessary to evolve slowly, that you cannot change your music overnight. Then I will say, "All right, but also try to bring forward the other life." Each time you make a successful attempt, feel, "My old life is coming to an end." Feel that you have got enough money, fame and so on. Even if you have not got enough, just try to convince your mind. In this way your soul will come forward. If you can make yourself feel that the whole world appreciates and admires you, that the whole world has given you what you want, but still you are not satisfied, then you will ask yourself what you still have to do in your life. What you have to do is to please your Inner Pilot in His own way.

Right now you may think that the world will not appreciate your spiritual music. It may take time, but today or tomorrow you will create another world of music. If you go on creating, one day people will appreciate your creation.

Inwardly the world wants to make progress. Outwardly the world wants something new. That which is eternal is outwardly new.

As a musician, when you want to offer something to the audience, if you use outer means all the time, you will not be able to give satisfaction. The world is always looking for the new. God Himself is looking for the new. This new river is flowing and we have to become one with the flow. Something new is coming out which offers progress to mankind, and if we become one with it, then we can really offer something to humanity.

Does humanity's interest in the performing arts help the world's progress?

Dance, theatre and music are meant to help the world's progress. Aspiration is bound to be followed by realisation, and realisation is bound to be followed by manifestation. If the performers do everything with a divine attitude to inspire and elevate the audience in some way, then certainly it helps the audience's progress. Otherwise, the wrong motive of the performers and the wrong motive of the audience cannot be of any help to the world's progress. Again, the inspiration that the audience gets today must be expanded tomorrow to a higher and deeper truth which we call aspiration.

When you are writing a poem or a song, do you sometimes invoke the soul of another great artist and use his capacities?

If you want to write like Shakespeare, if his soul is still in the soul's world and if you can invoke the soul and reach it, the soul may give you some of its capacities. This is absolutely true. Or if the person is still alive, you can also invoke the soul. But just by invoking the soul of a great writer or singer you cannot get his highest achievements. Before you sing, if you pray directly to the Supreme and say, "Now I am going to sing. I will be so grateful to You if You give me a most soulful voice like he has or she has," that is the most effective method. If you try to invoke the soul of someone who is a good singer, your mind may immediately think of his or her undivine qualities. You know that somebody sings well, but you may not be able to appreciate that particular person's inner life. You only appreciate a certain capacity which you want, but your physical mind is so bad that it will not allow you to separate the person's soul from his life on the physical plane. You want to think of the soul, but immediately the body may come before your mind. And when the body comes, immediately you think twenty bad things about the person, so you do not derive much help from him.

Pray to the Supreme, placing the Supreme in front of you. Say, "Supreme, I am praying to You to give me the singing capacity of so-and-so." At that time, you are putting the Supreme in between you and the other person whose excellent voice you want to have. Then you do get capacity, and this capacity will not be of any harm to you. But this does not mean that you will get the same height as the other person.

What is the spiritual essence of Beethoven's music?

The spiritual essence of Beethoven's music is that the outer life can be harmonised, liberated and fulfilled by the soul's conscious guidance of the physical in us. Even if the outer life starts from the darkest ignorance, it has hope. First it has hope, then it has the certainty of its total transformation, illumination and perfection.

When Beethoven's music starts, it gives the feeling of a mad elephant, first striking this side, then that side. We can imagine it striking one wall, then moving to the other side and striking another wall; but it is moving, moving—constant movement. Then the movement, after getting a few blows, after breaking heads here and there, goes toward the goal. Whether we call it soulful movement, vital movement or something else, it eventually reaches the goal.

What Beethoven says about music is true not only from the intellectual and emotional point of view, but also from the spiritual point of view: "Music is the mediator between the spiritual and the sensual life. Although the spirit be not master of that which it creates through music, yet it is blessed in this creation, which, like every creation of art, is mightier than the artist."

FOUR

The Soulful Singer

If you can sing divine songs
  Most soulfully,
You are bound to get the same results
As from your sublime meditation.

You sing songs with endless delight.
I sing songs while walking along
   The road of the ever-unknown.
You sing; therefore even in teeming darkness
   There is a candle flame that brightly shines.
I sing because You are my Eternity's comrade.

*S*inging immediately inspires us and awakens the slumbering soul in us. If we sing a divine song, a soulful song, it immediately brings purity into our system. Singing purifies our limited consciousness and brings to us universal Harmony. In our day-to-day life, we constantly break the universal Harmony, but when we sing, we build and create this universal Harmony in and around us.

If we can sing, we can have the purest consciousness and perfect harmony in our nature. Nothing delights our soul more than soulful singing.

When I sing, I try to communicate with God and offer Him what I have and what I am. In each song I sing, I try to offer myself through the song with utmost concern. The meaning of the words I try to convey through my voice. There are many singers who have extraordinary voices and singing ability. I am no match for them. But I have heard many singers of that type who do not feel the living breath of the words when they sing. Their beautiful, melodious voices carry the tune, but the depth and real significance of the words, we do not get from their voices.

Some people do not have a beautiful singing voice at all, but God deeply appreciates their voice because they sing soulfully. Someone may be a very great singer but sing without any aspiration or devotion. God cares most for the ones who sing soulfully.

When we chant, our psychic being, which is the representative of the soul, is fed. A mother feeds her child whenever the child is hungry. Similarly, we have to feed the soul, the divine child within us, by chanting or meditating. When the soul is constantly fed, it comes to the fore and the soul-bird gets the opportunity to fly in the sky of Infinity and Eternity.

When we sing, we have to become one with the inner singer. Outwardly we may be very expert in music, but if we do not have the capacity to become one with the inner singer, then our singing will not be soulful.

The song and the singer must be inseparable. When a singer sings spiritual songs, if he lives the song that he sings, then God will be a living Reality at every second. Otherwise, God will remain in the infinite blue sky and the singer will remain down on earth. Then there will be a yawning gulf between God's Feet and the singer's head.

When a seeker-singer sings soulfully, he immediately feels that he is immortal, or at least that he is going to stay on earth for many, many years. Again, when the same seeker-singer starts thinking teeming thoughts, the world of multifarious activities and problems enters into his mind and weakens it. At that time he sees that his death is fast approaching. So when he sings soulfully, he feels that he has become one with Immortality.

When you sing, you have to think of both the body of the song and the soul of the song. The body of the song is each word. You have to know the meaning of the song well and bring the image right in front of your mind.

If you can meditate for five minutes or ten minutes before you sing, then you will get the soul aspect of the song from your meditation. Even if you have not meditated, sometimes it is possible, while bringing the image of each word to your mind, to also get the soul aspect. But for this you have to be a great seeker.

If you bring the soul aspect forward and also symbolically bring the body aspect forward, the song becomes really soulful. At that time, those who are listening are bound to feel the soul inside the music. They may not even hear the words; they will only see the soul inside the song. They will see in your face the divine reality. Sometimes your soul has permeated your outer face, and your face is shining. At that time, they do not see anything but the soul.

Is it possible to feel our soul through meditation consisting of prolonged singing and chanting?

It is quite possible to see, feel and grow into the soul's light and reality through singing and chanting. It all depends on how you do it. While singing and chanting, if you look around to see whether others are appreciating your extraordinary voice, you will never be able to feel your soul. If you are watching to see how your voice is giving everybody tremendous joy in the form of a thrill, you have to know that this thrill is in the vital world of the audience. But if you are singing soulfully and devotedly, and if you feel at every moment that you are offering a flower of gratitude to the Supreme inside yourself, then you are bound to feel your soul. You have to feel that you have within yourself an endless supply of gratitude-flowers, and that at each second you are offering gratitude. If you can feel this, then you are bound to see the soul, feel the soul and grow into the soul's light and reality while singing and chanting.

Do souls sing?

Yes, souls do sing. But they do not have a tongue and a mouth like us. They sing with light and delight. Their way of communicating or expressing themselves is either through light or delight.

How can we keep the mind pure when we are not concentrating or meditating?

The best thing you can do is learn a few spiritual songs and sing them to yourself in silence while you are working or driving your car or doing anything that does not require mental concentration. While you are chanting in silence, your mind is being purified, because your soul is coming forward.

When you chant or sing, try to feel that the Supreme is listening. Otherwise, the chant will become a mere mechanical habit. Feel that there is a listener—not a human listener, but the Supreme Himself—listening inside your heart. When you feel that you have a divine listener, you will get more inspiration; you will be surcharged with boundless inspiration and endless inner joy. When you feel the presence of the Supreme inside your heart, you will be blessed with utmost joy and pride. He will do everything to transform, purify, illumine and liberate your mind.

I cannot sing. I sing in a monotone, and I cannot learn an instrument. Can I still create music?

The word 'creation' is a complicated term, and 'appreciation' is also a complicated thing. But creation and appreciation can be made very simple. Creation, when it is oneness with God's Will, need not be on the physical plane or the vital plane or the mental plane. It can be on God's own plane, through oneness with God. Suppose somebody has composed a beautiful piece of music. If you can identify yourself with the inner cry of the music, then you become a co-sharer, a co-creator. I always suggest that my students identify themselves with my songs, with my music and poetry. If they can do that, they have every right to feel that they have also composed these songs, that they also have written these poems, that they also created these paintings. It is one hundred percent true. On the physical plane, I used paper and pen, but that is immaterial. On the inner plane, the real creation is oneness.

When I sing, it sounds so horrible that it takes away my inspiration.

Singing is a form of meditation. If you cannot carry a tune, no harm. Then you will not sing in public. But certainly you can sing when you are alone.

The Supreme is not going to give you a bad mark if you cannot carry a tune. As long as you sing soulfully, the Supreme will be extremely pleased. Tagore once wrote in a poem, "You gave the bird a voice. To me you have not given a voice, but still I am singing." When you do not have something, and still you are offering it to God, God is very pleased with you. So try to sing in your own way. Even if the tune is wrong, if you sing soulfully, it is a real form of meditation. When I am singing and my voice is not good, or when I am playing a piece and I strike a wrong note, inside the wrong note I use my concentrative power to give my voice or music a sweetness, and that power enters into the audience. I am hearing the unsatisfactory notes, but the audience is hearing the sweetness, the subtle, delicate qualities. Sometimes their minds may know that I hit the wrong note, but inside that note they get tremendous joy: something new, something sweet.

Is it also a form of singing to hear the song in your mind?

Certainly. But when you sing outwardly, it convinces the outer mind. If you sing outwardly, you feel that there is a witness. If you do not complete the song, you will be embarrassed. If you sing in silence, then in the middle of the line you may stop and nobody will criticise you. But when you do it outwardly, at that time you feel that you will be exposed, that the ear is the witness.

Your songs are such an eternal flow. How can you tell when one begins and another ends?

In the inner world, my songs have neither beginning nor ending. Continuously I hear them. I have no idea where they come from, and I have no idea where they will end or whether they will end at all. But the songs that I compose with words do have a beginning and an ending. Anything that is done on the physical plane will have a beginning and an ending, whereas anything that is achieved or revealed on the inner plane has neither a beginning nor a culmination.

Anything that is on earth, anything that has been seen by the gross physical eyes, will always have a beginning and an ending. In any field of life there will be a beginning and a culmination if the thing touches the earth plane. Earth means limitation. But if it remains above the earth level, then it is beginningless and endless.

Music is meditation
If it is sung soulfully by good singers
Or even if it is sung badly by singers
With soulful hearts.

Not how you sing
But for Whom you sing
Is of supreme importance.

Sing a song soulfully.
Immediately from head to foot
    You will be flooded
With tremendous inner happiness,
And this happiness is true progress.

FIVE

Mantras and Chanting

Remembrance of God's Name
Is perfection-sky.
Repetition of God's Name
Is satisfaction-sun.

*I*n the inner life, mantras play a considerable role. A mantra is a syllable, group of syllables or a sentence divinely surcharged with power. This power can be utilised for a divine purpose or for an undivine purpose once it is attained through chanting. There are many, many Sanskrit mantras, and everybody has his own mantra. In the Indian scriptures it is said that if you want mental illumination, if you want purity, or if you want some other quality, then you should practise a mantra.

Japa

Japa is the repetition of a mantra. If you repeat Aum twice, thrice or hundreds of times, this repetition is japa. In true japa, the seeker has to repeat a particular mantra which is given to him by his Master. If he does not have a Master, then his mantra can be revealed from within. A seeker can also determine inwardly how many times he should repeat his mantra if he has no Master to tell him.

If a follower of Japa Yoga needs purity, the Master will tell him to repeat a particular mantra a few thousand times daily. If he needs mental knowledge, he will have to repeat a different mantra. For each divine quality the aspirant wants, he must chant a different mantra. The aspirant may have decided to repeat the name of God ten or fifteen thousand times, with the expectation of a certain result. But while he is chanting the name over and over again, he may actually be thinking of something else. The lack of one-pointed concentration and soulful attention while one is chanting takes away most of the effectiveness of the mantra. If you repeat the name of God ten thousand times while thinking of something else, you cannot expect to get any result. It does not matter how many hours you chant if you do not chant sincerely and soulfully. But if you do chant properly, then japa can be most effective.

Japa should not be done just before going to bed. If japa is done one thousand, two thousand or three thousand times, the mind will become agitated because the body wants to enter into the world of sleep. The aspirant will repeat "Supreme, Supreme, Supreme . . ." but he will only be working the mind like a machine. If he continues beyond his capacity, his mind will become agitated. Then he will suffer because he will not get proper sleep.

Japa may be done in the morning or during the day. But it should be done only one hundred or two hundred or at most three hundred times before going to bed. If you forget to do japa or do not feel like doing it during the day, and then do it all just before going to bed, this is very bad. If you meditate before going to bed you will invoke peace, light and bliss; but if you do japa one thousand times you will invoke power and energy and you will become too tense to sleep.

At times we will discover that we hear the word we have been repeating even after we stop. If we continue repeating "Supreme, Supreme, Supreme" for some time, when we stop, we will hear the same name of God being repeated inside our heart. The mouth is not functioning, but the inner being has started repeating the mantra naturally and spontaneously.

Japa is not, strictly speaking, a form of meditation. It is an invocation. By using a mantra, we can invoke God to enter into our inner existence, our inmost self. In meditation we try in a broader way to enter into God's Infinity, Eternity and Immortality.

Using Mantras

Each mantra offers a particular result. While using a mantra, we invoke a certain aspect of God to give us peace, light, bliss or something else that we want or need. If we can meditate well for ten or fifteen min—utes, this serves the same purpose, because we enter into the infinite expanse of peace, light and bliss, where our soul can drink whatever it needs or wants.

But when aspirants cannot enter into their deepest meditation because the mind is restless, this is their opportunity to use a mantra. 'Supreme', 'Aum', or 'God' can be repeated by anyone for a few minutes before starting meditation. The mantra should be repeated slowly and aloud. If you want quick results in your inner life, repeat a mantra every day without fail, for at least half an hour: fifteen minutes in the morning and fifteen minutes in the evening.

The Gayatri Mantra

Mantras are of two types. One is called *dhvani-antak*, which means 'with sound'. This mantra comes into existence from sound. The other kind is called *varnantak,* which means 'lettered'. This mantra is called a soundless mantra. When two things are struck together we hear a sound. But we hear the sound of Aum, the *anahata nada* or 'soundless sound', in the inmost recesses of our heart. *Ahata* means struck; *anahata* means unstruck. *Varnantak* and *anahata* are the same.

In India we have many mantras. In the *Bhagavad Gita*, Sri Krishna says that the Gayatri Mantra is the best. Its meaning is: "We meditate on the transcendental glory of the Deity Supreme, who is inside the heart of the earth, inside the life of the sky, and inside the soul of Heaven. May He stimulate and illumine our minds." It is said that if one can recite this special mantra one hundred thousand times, then all his wishes will be fulfilled. Any desire, any aspiration, no matter how mighty, will be fulfilled.

A Mantra for Health

If you are physically weak, if your physical constitution is not satisfactory, chant this mantra sincerely and soulfully:

> *Tejohasi tejomayi dhehi*
> *Viryamasi viryam mayi dhehi*
> *Valam masi valam mayi dhehi*

In a week's time you will see a change for the better in your health. It means:

> I pray for dynamic energy;
> I pray for dynamic virility;
> I pray for indomitable physical strength.

The Money Mantra

In this world some people are poor while others are rich. Some people are desperately in need of money to make both ends meet. Some years ago, a student of mine was having tremendous financial difficulties. I gave her a particular mantra:

Ya Devi sarvabhutesu
Ratna rupena sangstitha
Nastasvai namastvai
Namastvai namo namah

In thirteen days she came to me and said that her finances had tremendously improved. The meaning of this mantra is:

I bow and bow and again I bow to the Supreme Goddess who resides in all human beings in the form of material wealth and prosperity.

Many people have used this mantra in India. In her case it took only thirteen days for the mantra to accomplish its purpose. In someone else's case it may take three months or just three days. This particular mantra has tremendous power, but it is effective only for bringing material wealth.

Mantras from the Upanishads

If you want to remain in supreme Ecstasy and Delight all the time, then you will have to chant this particular mantra:

Anandadd hy eva khalv imani bhutani jayante
Anandena jatani jivanti
Anandam prayantyabhisam visanti

It means:

> From Delight we came into existence.
> In Delight we grow.
> At the end of our journey's close, into
> Delight we retire.

If Infinity is the particular object of your aspiration, if you want to have infinite Consciousness within and without, then the mantra that you have to practise is:

> *Purnam adah purnam idam*
> *purnat purnam udacyate*
> *Purnasya purnam adaya purnam*
> *evavasisyate*

It means:

> Infinity is that.
> Infinity is this.
> From Infinity, Infinity has come into
> existence.
> From Infinity, when Infinity is taken
> away, Infinity remains.

The Seed-Sounds of the Chakras

There are six major psychic centres in the human body. These centres are actually located in the subtle body. For each centre there is a seed-sound or mantra. Each word represents a state of consciousness, and within each state of consciousness there will be a particular symbol, perhaps a flower or an animal.

The centre at the base of the spine is called *Muladhara*. If an advanced seeker repeats the seed word *lam* while focusing all his attention at the base of the spine, in the course of time he will open this centre and he will be endowed with the power to cure diseases.

A few inches higher, near the spleen, is the *Svadhisthana* centre. He who repeats the mantra *vam* while concentrating on this centre will eventually be endowed with the power to offer love to everyone and everything and to receive love from everyone and everything.

He who concentrates on the *Manipura* or navel centre and repeats the syllable *ram* with power and force will eventually be able to conquer all sorrow and suffering. Also, this centre gives the power to enter into the subtle worlds and higher planes.

The mantra *yam* is to be chanted slowly and sweetly in the heart centre, *Anahata*. He who opens the heart centre attains pure joy and the bliss of oneness.

He who chants *ham* while concentrating on the throat centre, *Vishuddha*, will receive the power of eloquence in expression in all forms of art.

The *Ajna* chakra is in the middle of the forehead, a little above the base of the nose. There the seed-word is *Aum*. By concentrating on this centre and chanting *Aum*, an advanced seeker can get boundless psychic and occult powers.

The *Sahasrara chakra* at the crown of the head is considered to be the seventh spiritual centre, although it is not linked to the other six. When one enters into this crown centre, one enters into trance and goes beyond the consciousness of this world. The mantra of this centre is *Supreme*.

The Musical Notes of the Chakras

The universal Consciousness embodies universal Music. From each chakra, where the life-energy from the universal Consciousness gathers, a musical note is produced. From *Sahasrara* the tone of *shadja* or *sa* is produced. In Western music you call this 'do'. From *Ajna, rishava* or *ri* is produced: what you call 're'. From *Vishuddha, gandhara* or *ga* is produced: what you call 'mi'. From *Anahata, madhyama* or *ma* is produced: what you call 'fa'. From *Manipura, panchama* or *pa* is produced: what you call 'so'. From *Svadhisthana, dhaivata* or *dha* is produced: what you call 'la'. From *Muladhara, nishada* or *ni* is produced: what you call 'ti'.

Use Mantras with Caution

I want to make it very clear that the opening of the chakras does not mean that one is realising God or that he is about to realise God. Not at all! From the highest spiritual point of view, the opening of the chakras is like the games a mother plays with her children in the playground. The mother knows the games will amuse her children.

If the centres are opened without proper purification, the seeker will encounter great pain. It will be like playing with fire or a sharp knife. He may destroy others or he himself may be destroyed. All real spiritual Masters say that it is better to open the heart centre first and then try to open the other centres. If one opens the heart centre first, there is practically no risk. But if one starts with the third eye or the lower chakras, it is very dangerous. If one opens up the lower chakras without the purification of the vital, especially the lower vital, then one can become unbalanced, mad, insane. It is like giving a knife to a child.

He may misuse it, cutting his finger or doing something most harmful and damaging. But if one is grown up and mature, then he will use the knife to cut fruit and offer it to his friends.

How quickly does a mantra remove desire from the mind?

It depends on the individual seeker. If he has established abundant purity in his being, then it is a matter of months. But if the seeker is not pure enough, the mantra may take a very long time to produce the necessary effect.

Is there a spiritual centre for creative expression, and should we concentrate on it before we create?

The throat chakra is the spiritual centre for art. If you can open this centre, then you can be a very good musician or a very good artist of any kind. All kinds of artistic capacities can be developed from this centre. The difficulty is that if your nature is not pure, then if you open this centre and become a great artist it will be all for name and fame, and all your aspiration will go away. When you open the throat centre, if your navel centre and lower centres are not properly purified, then as soon as you create something, worldly appreciation will lower your consciousness. It may happen that you will only create for world applause and not with the idea of serving God through your creation. If you cannot have the inner assurance of purity, the best thing is to pray to the Supreme to purify you and illumine your consciousness so that you will not fall from the spiritual life when you get boundless artistic capacity by opening this chakra. But if you have consciously established a certain standard of peace, light and bliss in your life, then you can safely open this centre and create something beautiful, meaningful and everlasting.

Is it only the throat chakra that enables us to become artists or musicians?

If you concentrate on the throat chakra, you will be able to become a very good artist, musician, writer, dancer or singer. This does not mean that the other centres do not have the capacity to help you in this way, but the throat centre has the utmost capacity. When you sing, you may feel an awakening in the throat centre. Those who have good voices have, to some extent, opened their throat centre. This is a very good experience.

Whoever has mastery over the throat chakra has the capacity to offer divine messages to the world. We get messages from various planes of consciousness.

But when one gets a message from the throat chakra, the message is sublime and everlasting. When this centre is open, one receives direct messages from the Highest and becomes a mouthpiece for the Highest. One becomes a poet, a singer or an artist. All forms of art are expressed from this centre.

SIX

Aum:

The Mother of All Mantras

Aum bhur bhuvah svah
Tat savitur varenyam
Bhargo devasya dhimahi
Dhiyo yo nah pracodayat

We meditate on the transcendental glory
of the Deity Supreme, who is inside the heart
of the earth, inside the life of the sky, and
inside the soul of Heaven. May He stimulate
and illumine our minds.

*T*here can be no mantra more powerful than the mother of all mantras, Aum, the cosmic sound. A yogi or spiritual figure hears it self-generated in the inmost recesses of his heart. When you begin to hear it, you can be certain that you are far advanced in the spiritual life. Your God-realisation will no longer remain a mere cry in the wilderness. The day of your Self-realisation is fast approaching.

We call Aum *anahata nada*, the unstruck or soundless sound. We use the word 'soundless', but that word is an infinite understatement. The cosmic sound is inaudible to the ordinary ears, but if we hear the soundless sound inside our heart, it is infinitely more powerful than the loudest sound we can produce. In softness there can be the greatest dynamism. Sometimes I talk in a fatherly way, with utmost concern and affection. I am talking in a very soft, delicate voice, but at that time I am using my absolutely most dynamic power. I may be smiling and offering all kinds of affection, but in my softness there is volcanic power.

If you repeat the word Aum every day for two, three or four hours, you will get the vibration of that sound within your heart. You will not have to create this sound inwardly, but by repeating Aum outwardly, the inner sound automatically comes. When the soundless sound is vibrating constantly in your heart, your whole body is surcharged with divine knowledge, divine light, divine power. If you practise only that mantra, that is enough to take you to God.

Aum is the symbol of God, the Supreme. It is God's sound. Every second God is creating Himself anew inside Aum. This sound He uses to create the world; this sound He uses to preserve the world; this sound He uses to transform the world.

Aum is the soundless sound. It is the vibration of the Supreme. It is a single, indivisible, ineffable sound. When we hear the soundless sound within, when we identify with it, when we live within it, we can be freed from the fetters of ignorance and realise the Supreme within and without.

When we chant Aum, what actually happens is that we bring down peace and light from above and create a universal harmony within and without us. When we repeat Aum, both our inner and our outer beings become inspired and surcharged with divine light and aspiration. Aum has no equal. Aum has infinite power. Just by repeating Aum, we can realise God.

When you chant Aum, try to feel that God is climbing up and down within you. Hundreds of seekers in India have realised God simply by repeating Aum. No matter how grave one's sin is, if one chants

Aum a few times from the depth of one's heart, God's omnipotent Compassion will forgive and redeem the seeker. In the twinkling of an eye, the power of Aum transforms darkness into light, ignorance into knowledge and death into Immortality.

How to Chant Aum

There are various ways to chant Aum. When we chant Aum with tremendous soul's power, what we actually do is enter into the cosmic vibration where the creation is in perfect harmony and where the cosmic Dance is being danced by the Absolute. If we chant Aum soulfully, we become one with the cosmic Dance; we become one with God the Creator, God the Preserver and God the Transformer. Aum is at once the Life, the Body and the Breath of God. This is what you can feel when you chant Aum.

If you get an attack on the emotional vital plane and wrong thoughts, wrong ideas, wrong vibrations enter into you, repeat Aum or the name of the Supreme as fast as possible. Do not chant slowly. When you are trying to cleanse your mind of impurities, you must chant as if you were running to catch a moving train.

When you do japa, do not prolong your chanting too much. If you prolong the syllable Aum, you will not have the time to chant five hundred or six hundred times. Just say the syllable in a normal but soulful way so that you will get the vibration. Practise it aloud, not silently. Let the sound of the mantra vibrate even in your physical ears and permeate your entire body.

We chant Aum aloud because when the outer mind is convinced, we get greater joy and a greater sense of achievement. But if we know how to enter into the original source of the sound, which is inside the heart, then we need not chant aloud. It is quite possible to utter the word Aum silently or to hear it inwardly without actually saying it. Wherever we are, the sound of Aum is already there. We can very often hear the sound of Aum without chanting it ourselves, but we do not know whether it is coming from our heart or from the atmosphere.

Sometimes during meditation seekers hear the sound of Aum although nobody is chanting it aloud. This means that inwardly somebody has chanted or is chanting Aum and the meditation room has preserved the sound. If we are conscious during sleep, we will hear the sound of Aum. It is not the heartbeat we will hear, but the soundless sound. We will hear it and feel it most convincingly.

If you want to meditate while you are in some public place where there is all kinds of noise, try to enter into your own inner sound itself. To your surprise, you will see that the sounds which disturbed you one minute ago do not bother you now. On the contrary, you will get a sense of achievement because instead of hearing noise, you will hear divine music, and that divine music is produced within you.

Is it helpful to chant Aum before meditating?

Chanting Aum before meditation is not at all necessary, but if one wants to get inspiration, it can be helpful. When we begin our meditation, we can first feel that we are entering into God the Creator who is creating aspiration in us. Then we can feel that God the Preserver is preserving us to continue our divine journey. Finally, we can feel that God the Transformer is transforming our ignorance into wisdom at every moment.

Aum is not a term which is meaningful to us in our culture.

True. In your culture the most significant word is 'God'. In India, we repeat Aum or the name of a cosmic god or goddess, like Shiva or Kali. In chanting a mantra the most important thing is to know in what aspect of the Supreme we have absolute faith. I use the word 'God' here in the West because I know that all your life you have been trained to pray to God. But Aum can also enter into you with all its significance. The time will come when you can go deeper within, and if Aum inspires you more than 'God', then you should chant Aum. It is the inspiration that you get which is of the utmost importance. You can chant the word 'God' if that gives you more inspiration.

SEVEN

Listening with the Heart

When we sing,
We embody and become
   The power of music.
This power has a free access
   To the Universal Heart.

Let us not try to understand music
    With our mind.
Let us not even try to feel it
    With our heart.
Let us simply and spontaneously
    Allow the music-bird to fly
In our heart-sky.
    While flying, it will unconditionally
Reveal to us
    What it has and what it is.
What it has
    Is Immortality's message
And what it is
    Is Eternity's passage.

*G*od's Music is heard by each individual according to his own capacity of receptivity. God plays the same Music, but it sounds one way to one person and totally different to another. When a professor gives a talk, there will be many students in the same classroom. Each student will understand the pro–fessor's talk differently. Because of his inner capacity, the best student in the class will understand much more than the worst student. God's Music is heard, valued, understood and felt in a specific way according to the listener's own capacity of receptivity.

God has created two kinds of music-lovers. One kind will try to study and understand music, most of the time on a mental level. These music-lovers enjoy music in a mental way. Again, there are some seekers who have no musical training, but they seek the music that is deep within. They enjoy music in a psychic way. The music that they hear at times far surpasses the music that others study.

If you can identify yourself with music, at that time you become the source, the composer. Also, when you listen to spiritual music and identify your–self with the singers, if the music is being sung very soulfully, this is nothing short of your own prayer and meditation.

How can we learn to hear the inner music?

Through constant prayer and meditation we can learn to hear the inner music. We have to pray soulfully to God to grant us light, abundant light, so that when we dive deep within we can hear His Message without being hindered by our doubting mind. The deeper we can dive, the sooner our doubting mind will leave us for good. So it is through prayer that we can listen to the dictates of our soul, dictates that embody music pristine in purity, light and delight.

What is the best way to become one with soulful music?

The best way to become one with soulful music is to have the firm inner conviction that while you are breathing in, the breath is immediately entering directly into your soul. And with the breath, you have to feel that the Universal Consciousness, divine Reality, divine Truth is also entering. Then, when you breathe out, try to feel that you are breathing out the ignorance that is covering your soul. Feel that the veils of ignorance are being lifted and discarded. If you can consciously imagine and feel this, it is the best way to become one with soulful music.

What role will music play in bringing about world oneness?

Music will play a most important role in bringing about world oneness, for music embodies the Universal Heart, the oneness-heart. Music transcends the barriers of nations, nationalities and religions. Music embodies universal light and universal truth, and music also embodies the oneness-reality which we see in universal love, universal light, universal awareness and universal wakefulness. Universal wakefulness we see inside all music. Music has to play a most important role in bringing about world oneness, for music is the connecting link between the One and the many and between the many and the One.

It is through music that the universal feeling of oneness can be achieved in the twinkling of an eye.

I was at a concert and I felt a connection with the violinist.

In this case you established your own inner oneness with the Source in him. On the outer plane he was playing; on the inner plane the soul was playing in and through you. You were entering into that particular musician; he was entering into the Source. From there the music was being played. It happens quite a few times when a seeker in the audience enters into the Source. The seeker who is in the audience can easily establish his oneness with the Source if he feels that he is being utilised by the Source. One is active; the other one is silent. The one that is playing is active and you at that time are silent. You are not merely a silent listener, but a silent participant.

EIGHT

Music from the Mountaintops:
The Heights of Consciousness

His soulful music expressed
His aspiration,
  His realisation
    And his oneness
With the Universal Consciousness.

God's favourite sound
   Is the sound of His inner Music.
This inner Music
Is the music of earth's transformation
   And humanity's life-perfection.

*I*t is quite possible to be both a musician and a Yogi. In Mother India there have been many saints, sages and spiritual Masters who were blessed with divine music. Their musical talent did not interfere with their God-realisation, and even after achieving God-realisation, their musical talents did not leave them.

Yoga means union, inseparable oneness with God. A Yogi is one who has established conscious union with God. He can easily become a musician because in his inseparable oneness with God, he can do anything he wants. But a Yogi has to wait for God's Will. If it is God's Will, he will become a musician; or if it is God's Will, he will become something else. Otherwise, he will just remain with his own lofty realisation and oneness; he will reveal and manifest the highest Peace, Light and Truth the way the Supreme wants him to.

When an individual realises God, he and God are not different beings; they are one, like a tiny drop and the vast ocean. In the same way, sometimes the soul responds to music. The soul thrills to music; it just melts and becomes one.

A Yogi's qualities and a musician's qualities can go side by side, provided the Yogi has the capacity and inherent talent for music. Even if the Yogi spends a very short time in the musical world, he can be a very good musician, but it will take infinitely more time for a musician to become a Yogi.

Spiritual Masters who have musical capacity can eventually show the world at large that inner music can be played outwardly and appreciated by the world. Inner music one can hear and one can create while one is meditating. We can hear inner music through aspiration. What is inner music? We have learned from the Indian Vedas that this music is the mother tongue of humanity, the language of the soul. It is through music that the Divine in us gets the opportunity to manifest itself here on earth.

When a musician's spiritual capacity becomes most powerful, he does not even have to speak. Others will just look at his face and see some illumination.

When a spiritual Master plays his music, through his music he enters into the heart and soul of the audience. At the same time, he is bringing down light from above. He is not just playing on an instrument. He is receiving something from the higher world and then offering it to the world at large. In an hour, thousands of people can feel this higher light as their very own. So music has the opportunity, the capacity, to claim the universe as its very own.

Music and Religion

Music and religion are like the obverse and reverse of the same reality-coin. Music in its purest sense is religion and religion in its purest sense is music. This music-religion, this code of life, this universal language of the soul, can only be offered; it cannot be purchased or sold. Music and religion are for the seekers, for the music-lovers, for the truth-servers. Money-power or earthly name and fame cannot lord it over these two immortal realities, these two earthly and heavenly treasures.

The source of true music and the source of true religion will always remain the same, and that source is a cry, a birthless and deathless cry—an eternal hunger. It is a hunger not for one's own satisfaction, but for God's Satisfaction in God's own way. When music and religion come from this source, only then will the message and beauty of music and the message and beauty of religion be divinely illumining and fulfilling.

The Story of Akbar, Tansen and Haridas

The Mogul Emperor Akbar employed the great musician Tansen in his court. One day when Akbar was deeply appreciating Tansen, Tansen said, "I am not a great musician."

Akbar said, "You are not only a great musician; you are the best musician."

But Tansen said, "No, my Guru, my teacher, Haridas, is by far the best."

The Emperor said, "Then bring him to my palace!"

Tansen replied, "No, he will not come. He does not care for name and fame. He plays only for God. God's Compassion is his sole reward."

Akbar said, "Then I will have to go to him. Take me to him."

Tansen agreed, but he told Akbar, "You cannot go as the Emperor. You have to go in the guise of my servant, my slave."

So Akbar went to Tansen's teacher as a servant, and Tansen begged his teacher to play for Akbar. Unfortunately, Haridas was not in the mood to play. Then a brilliant idea struck Tansen's mind. He started playing, deliberately making many mistakes. Haridas could not believe his eyes and ears. How could his best student make such deplorable mistakes? Out of great surprise and shock, he started playing in order to correct his student. In this way the Emperor came to realise that Tansen's teacher was indeed far superior to Tansen.

When they came back to the palace, Akbar asked Tansen, "How is it that you cannot play as soulfully as your teacher does?"

Tansen replied, "I play for name and fame. I play for you. He plays for God. Here is the difference. If I played for God—for God in you, for God in every-one—only then would my music be supernatural, heavenly, supremely soulful and perfect. But I play for money-power, for name and fame. How do you expect me to play the way my teacher does?"

Can spiritual music inspire non-spiritual listeners?

Spiritual music can inspire non-spiritual listeners in the same way that God inspires unaspiring humanity. In the beginning there was darkness; then there was light. Because God has always inspired unaspiring humanity, this light is continually increasing. If some individuals are not aspiring right now, it is the bounden duty of those who are already awakened to inspire them in the same way that the Supreme, out of His infinite bounty, inspired and continues to inspire the ones who are now well established in the world of aspiration.

Each individual has a heart. Spirituality is in the heart, with the heart and for the heart. It is only a matter of time before the heart responds to spiritual music, which embodies the beauty and purity of music in its pristine form and in infinite measure.

A great musician can add to the inner cry of the person who practises a spiritual life. And if the musician himself believes in God wholeheartedly, then his music can be of tremendous help to his own spiritual practice.

What do you concentrate on when you play music?

Most of the time I concentrate on the soul of the particular piece that I am playing. Each song has a soul, so I concentrate on the soul of each song. Sometimes I concentrate on the soul of a particular melody that I feel is very haunting; and I try to reveal and manifest the divine beauty of that melody.

You have created thousands of paintings, poems and songs. Where does this endless fountain of creativity come from?

This endless fountain of creativity comes from only one Source, and that Source I call the unconditional Compassion of my Lord Beloved Supreme. He bestows upon me His unconditional Compassion-Light and according to my receptivity He creates in and through me.

Is there art in other worlds besides earth?

Yes, there is art in other worlds and other planes of consciousness apart from earth, but this art is not for manifestation. This art is something that exists for its own sake. It comes spontaneously. Here on earth, whenever we do something, even if we just exist, we do it for the sake of others. A tree has flowers and fruits. Even if the tree does not want to give me anything, still I can climb up its trunk and eat its fruits or pluck its flowers, or I can just enjoy its shade if I want to. But in the other worlds it is not like that. There you can appreciate the beauty of something, but you cannot claim it or use it for your own purpose. Here on earth, as soon as art is created, you can steal it with force or buy it or plead with the artist to give it to you. In the other worlds, you can at most appreciate it, but you cannot capture the art, you cannot claim it, you cannot acquire it, because it is not manifested.

In other worlds you see the *Gandharvas*—the celestial musicians like Narada, who is the most prominent one. There is a particular world where a constant assembly of musicians is held. There is also a world for artists in the inner world. There are some artists who have not taken incarnation but just remain in this inner world. Again, some great artists, spiritual artists from earth, go to this world to enjoy it when they leave the body.

O Master-Musician,
Tune me for life again.
The awakening of new music
  My heart wants to become.
My life is now mingled
  In ecstasy's height.

NINE

God the Supreme Musician

God the Supreme Musician
  Offers His Music of Peace.
Man the divine audience
  Offers his peace-receptivity.

My earth-songs
Devotedly find me.

My Heaven-songs
Soulfully illumine me.

My God-songs
Triumphantly immortalise me.

*G*od is the Supreme Musician. It is He who is playing with us, on us and in us. We cannot separate God from His Music. The universal Consciousness is constantly being played by the Supreme Himself, and is constantly growing into the supreme Music. God the Creator is the Supreme Musician and God the creation is the supreme Music. The Musician and His Music can never be separated. His creation is being fulfilled. The Music supreme feels its fulfilment only when it consciously becomes one with the Supreme, the Creator Himself. Through music, God is offering the message of unity in multiplicity and also the message of multiplicity in unity.

Music is God's Dream. God is dreaming at every moment through music. His Dream is called the cosmic Reality, the universal Reality. From the highest point of view, music is not mere words; it is not a concept, not an idea. Music is Reality in its highest form. God is playing the supreme Music in and through us, His chosen instruments. He is playing on us in His own Way. He does not need any human instruments or words to convey His Message, to convey Himself. This He can do in silence without taking any help from the sound-world. God created sound in order to know outwardly what He is inwardly. Inwardly He knows what He is, but if He does not outwardly manifest His inner Divinity then the world cannot accept Him, cannot realise Him. So He created sound just for the sake of His own manifestation.

God-Music purifies our body.
God-Music strengthens our soul.
God-Music expedites our life-liberation,
    God-realisation and love-manifestation.

Be a pioneer
In God's Music-World.
Your dedication-life
    Can offer God-Music
To many receptive hearts.

God's Music
Comes from God's Heart
  Of Silence-Delight.

God's Songs
Come from God's Eye
  Of Compassion-Love.

EPILOGUE

Master Musicians:

Interviews with Pablo Casals and Leonard Bernstein

As there are two kinds of music—silence-music and sound-music—even so there are two kinds of musicians: musicians with genius and musicians with talent. Once a young student went to the great composer Mozart and asked Mozart to teach him how to write a concerto. The great composer told him to wait for a few more years before attempting to write a concerto. The young student reminded the great musician that he had been only eight or nine when he started composing such marvelous pieces. Mozart replied that when he was a child, he did not have to go to anyone for advice. Since the young student needed to ask someone else how to write a concerto, Mozart's advice was for him to wait a few years. So here we see the difference between a musician with boundless genius and a musician with ordinary talent.

Excerpts from a meeting with Pablo Casals, 5 October 1972, in Don Pablo's studio in Puerto Rico.

Sri Chinmoy: I am offering you my deepest love plus admiration for what you have done for humanity through your music. It is just like you are lifting the veil of ignorance. And only music can please God more than anything else because God Himself is the Supreme Musician. Each player—each instrument—in God's Cosmic Game is unique, and God is playing a different note on each instrument. So each soul is a unique manifestation of God.

Don Pablo: I see in the melody of Nature, God. It is a wonderful work of art. The spirit of the art is wonderful. And I feel that I am myself because I have never taken music lightly.

Sri Chinmoy: You take music as prayer, constant inner prayer to bring down the highest Light from above. You do not take music as a vocation, as ordinary people do. In your case, music has been your prayer, your meditation, your oneness with Nature, with God. Earth is God in manifestation.

Don Pablo: Music is a manifestation of God like everything else.

Sri Chinmoy: I wish to say that you are a most developed, mature spiritual soul. The world knows you, has recognised you as the greatest musician. But a day will come in your future incarnations when the world will recognise you as a spiritual Master also because your soul is now ready to launch into the spiritual life. And in your future incarnations also you will do the most splendid work. That is to say, you will do something unique in manifesting the eternal God, God's Light, through your creation.

You are the real creator of music, and to the creator I offer my deepest love and gratitude. You are the eternal child of God. Each time you play on your instrument, it is a new creation—you create God and manifest God in a unique way. Each time you touch your cello, you bring a new life into existence. And this life is the divine Life that comes directly from Heaven through your music.

Don Pablo (after meditating with Sri Chinmoy): I am most grateful to you for the most wonderful moment of my life.

Sri Chinmoy: It has been the most wonderful moment in my life, too. I am so happy to see you. You cannot imagine how happy, how delighted, how proud I am to see you, because in you I see a real seeker of the infinite Truth, who is trying to manifest divinity through music. And the aspiring world is accepting divinity from you, from your dedicated work. Please feel my deepest gratitude. You have done and you will be doing so much for mankind.

One last thing, I was telling your wife that most musicians learn music and play mechanically. They become experts in a mechanical way. In your case, it is not something mechanical. Your music and God are totally, inseparably one; one cannot be separated from the other. You cannot separate God from music, so God is constantly revealing Himself through your music. When you think of music, God is there; when you think of God, music is there.

Don Pablo: Yes, that is what I feel. Bless you, bless you, bless you. Thank you, thank you, thank you.

Excerpts from an interview with Leonard Bernstein on 21 March 1979 in New York.

Sri Chinmoy: You are the ocean of music, and inside your music-world the world of aspiration and dedication is constantly growing.

(Sri Chinmoy and Leonard Bernstein meditate together.)

Leonard Bernstein: I haven't done that in so long. I was taught to meditate about four years ago. I did it as strictly as I could for seven weeks. But I couldn't continue it, so I lost it. Every once in a while I would come back to it. My mantra was always with me. But I haven't done it for a very long time, and you brought that back.

Sri Chinmoy: You have offered to the world at large something unique, and the outer world knows who you are because of the magnificence of your unique contribution. The golden day will dawn when the supreme message which you embody in the inner world will come to the fore. At that time the world will see you as the supreme seeker who is also the supreme composer and conductor. God the Lover-aspect, which you embody in boundless measure, has yet to come to the fore.

Leonard Bernstein: I don't know how many years more I have to do that. That worries me, because I do have a lot to do. You're right. I've only begun, but I am sixty years old.

Sri Chinmoy: In the Heart of our Beloved Supreme, sixty years is nothing. It is a fleeting second. The promise that your soul has made to the Supreme you are bound to fulfil. Your soul will not be satisfied unless and until you have offered to the world at large everything that you are supposed to offer and everything that you are.

(Sri Chinmoy's students sing a song he composed for the occasion in honour of Leonard Bernstein.)

Leonard Bernstein: What music I hear! Beautiful. He has no idea he is writing counterpoint. *(To Sri Chinmoy)* If I say 'counterpoint' to you, you will ask what that is. *(To the group)* But he has written a counterpoint like Bach. Every phrase goes with every other phrase, so that no matter what you do, you cannot miss. My musical spirit is very, very deeply impressed.

ABOUT THE AUTHOR

SRI CHINMOY is a fully realised spiritual Master dedicated to serving those seeking a deeper meaning in life. Through his teaching of meditation, his music, art and writings, his athletics and his own life of dedicated service to humanity, he tries to inspire others to find inner peace and fulfilment.

Born in Bengal in 1931, Sri Chinmoy entered an ashram (spiritual community) at the age of 12. His life of intense spiritual practice included meditating for up to 14 hours a day, together with writing poetry, essays and devotional songs, doing selfless service and practising athletics. While still in his early teens, he had many profound inner experiences and attained spiritual realisation. He remained in the ashram for 20 years, deepening and expanding his realisation, and in 1964 came to New York City to share his inner wealth with sincere seekers.

Today, Sri Chinmoy serves as a spiritual guide to disciples in more than 100 centres around the world. He advocates the path of the heart as the simplest way to make rapid spiritual progress. By meditating on the spiritual heart, he teaches, the seeker can discover his own inner treasures of peace, joy, light and love. The role of a spiritual Master, according to Sri Chinmoy, is to help the seeker live so that these inner riches can

illumine his life. He instructs his disciples in the inner
life and elevates their consciousness not only beyond
their expectation, but even beyond their imagination.
In return he asks his students to meditate regularly
and to try to nurture the inner qualities he brings to
the fore in them.

Sri Chinmoy teaches that love is the most direct
way for a seeker to approach the Supreme. When a
child feels love for his father, it does not matter how
great the father is in the world's eye; through his love
the child feels only his oneness with his father and his
father's possessions. This same approach, applied to
the Supreme, permits the seeker to feel that the
Supreme and His Eternity, Infinity and Immortality
are the seeker's own. This philosophy of love, Sri
Chinmoy feels, expresses the deepest bond between
man and God, who are aspects of the same unified
consciousness. In the life-game, man fulfils himself in
the Supreme by realising that God is his own highest
self. The Supreme reveals Himself through man, who
serves as His instrument for world transformation
and perfection.

In the traditional Indian fashion, Sri Chinmoy
does not charge a fee for his spiritual guidance, nor
does he charge for his frequent concerts or public
meditations. His only fee, he says, is the seeker's
sincere inner cry. He takes a personal interest in each

of his students, and when he accepts a disciple, he takes full responsibility for that seeker's inner progress. In New York, Sri Chinmoy meditates in person with his disciples several times a week and offers a regular weekly evening meditation session for the general public. Students living outside New York see Sri Chinmoy during worldwide gatherings that take place three times a year, during visits to New York, or during the Master's frequent trips to their cities. They find that the inner bond between Master and disciple transcends physical separation.

Sri Chinmoy accepts students at all levels of development, from beginners to advanced seekers, and lovingly guides them inwardly and outwardly according to their individual needs.

Sri Chinmoy personally leads an active life, demonstrating most vividly that spirituality is not an escape from the world, but a means of transforming it. He has written more than 1000 books, which include plays, poems, stories, essays, commentaries and answers to questions on spirituality. He has painted thousands of widely exhibited mystical paintings and composed more than 14,000 devotional songs. Performing his own compositions on a wide variety of instruments, he has offered a series of several hundred Peace Concerts in cities around the world.

A naturally gifted athlete and a firm believer in the spiritual benefits of physical fitness, Sri Chinmoy encourages his disciples to participate in sports. Under his inspirational guidance, the international Sri Chinmoy Marathon Team organises hundreds of road races, including the longest certified race in the world (3,100 miles), and stages a biennial global relay run for peace.

For further information, please write to:
AUM PUBLICATIONS
86-10 Parsons Blvd.
Jamaica, NY 11432

ADDITIONAL TITLES
by Sri Chinmoy

GOD is...
Selected Writings of Sri Chinmoy

This long-awaited book gathers Sri Chinmoy's insights about God into one volume. These selections are drawn from the more than one thousand books he has written in over thirty years of teaching spirituality and meditation. His intimate knowledge of God transcends religious dogma and scripture, shedding light on all seekers' paths to God. The simplicity of the language belies an astonishing depth of knowledge that goes beyond the intellect and directly communicates the wisdom of the soul.

Topics include: Can the existence of God be proven? • The cause of your separation from God • Should you ever fear God? • Seeing God in all • The meaning of suffering • Increasing your need for God • How to know what God wants you to do with your life. $12.95

The Three Branches of India's Life-Tree:
Commentaries on the Vedas, the Upanishads and the Bhagavad Gita

This book brings together in one volume Sri Chinmoy's commentaries on the Vedas, the Upanishads and the Bhagavad Gita, three ancient Indian scriptures which are the foundations of Hindu spiritual tradition. His approach is clear and practical, and at the same time profound and richly poetic. In a style unmistakably his own, Sri Chinmoy makes direct and personal contact with the reader, who joins him on a journey through the wisdom of these celebrated classics. This book is both an excellent introduction for readers who are coming to the subject for the first time, and a series of illumining meditations for those who already know it well. $13.95

Meditation: Man-Perfection in God-Satisfaction

Presented with the simplicity and clarity that have become the hallmark of Sri Chinmoy's writings, this book is easily one of the most comprehensive guides to meditation available.

Topics include: Proven meditation techniques that anyone can learn • How to still the restless mind • Developing the power of concentration • Carrying peace with you always • Awakening the heart centre to discover the power of your soul • The significance of prayer. Plus a special section in which Sri Chinmoy answers questions on a wide range of experiences often encountered in meditation. $9.95

Beyond Within:
A Philosophy for the Inner Life

"How can I carry on the responsibilities of life and still grow inwardly to find spiritual fulfilment?"

When your simple yearning to know the purpose of your life and feel the reality of God has you swimming against the tide, then the wisdom and guidance of a spiritual Master who has crossed these waters is priceless. Sri Chinmoy offers profound insight into man's relationship with God, and sound advice on how to integrate the highest spiritual aspirations into daily life.

Topics include: The transformation and perfection of the body • The spiritual journey • Meditation • The relationship between the mind and physical illness • Using the soul's will to conquer life's problems • How you can throw away guilt • Overcoming fear of failure • The purpose of pain and suffering • Becoming conscious of your own divine nature • The occult. $13.95

Death and Reincarnation

This deeply moving book has brought consolation and understanding to countless people faced with the loss of a loved one or fear of their own mortality. Sri Chinmoy explains the secrets of death, the afterlife and reincarnation.

$7.95

Kundalini: The Mother-Power

En route to his own spiritual realisation, Sri Chinmoy attained mastery over the Kundalini and occult powers. In this book he explains techniques for awakening the Kundalini and the chakras. He warns of the dangers and pitfalls to be avoided and discusses some of the occult powers that come with the opening of the chakras. $7.95

Yoga and the Spiritual Life

Specifically tailored for Western readers, this book offers rare insight into the philosophy of Yoga and Eastern mysticism.

It offers novices as well as advanced seekers a deep understanding of the spiritual side of life. Of particular interest is the section on the soul and the inner life. $8.95

The Summits of God-Life:
Samadhi and Siddhi
A genuine account of the
world beyond time and space

This is Sri Chinmoy's firsthand account of states of consciousness that only a handful of Masters have ever experienced. Not a theoretical or philosophical book, but a vivid and detailed description of the farthest possibilities of human consciousness. Essential reading for all seekers longing to fulfil their own spiritual potential. $8.95

Inner and Outer Peace
A powerful yet simple approach for establishing
peace in your own life and the world

Sri Chinmoy speaks of the higher truths that energise the quest for world peace, giving contemporary expression to the relationship between our personal search for inner peace and the world's search for outer peace. He reveals truths which lift the peace of the world above purely political and historical considerations, contributing his spiritual understanding and inspiration to the cause of world peace. $7.95

A Child's Heart and a Child's Dreams
Growing Up with Spiritual Wisdom—A Guide for Parents and Children

Sri Chinmoy offers practical advice on a subject that is not only an idealist's dream but every concerned parent's lifeline: fostering your child's spiritual life, watching him or her grow up with a love of God and a heart of self-giving.

Topics include: Ensuring your child's spiritual growth • Education and spirituality—their meeting ground • Answers to children's questions about God • A simple guide to meditation and a special section of children's stories guaranteed to delight and inspire. $7.95

The Master and the Disciple

What is a Guru? There are running gurus, diet gurus and even stock market gurus. But to those in search of spiritual enlightenment, the Guru is not merely an 'expert'; he is the way to their self-realisation. Sri Chinmoy says in this definitive book on the Guru-disciple relationship: "The most important thing a Guru does for his spiritual children is to make them aware of something vast and infinite within themselves, which is nothing other than God Himself."

Topics include: How to find a Guru • Telling a real spiritual Master from a false one • How to recognise your own Guru • Making the most spiritual progress while under the guidance of a spiritual Master • What it means when a Guru takes on your karma • Plus a special section of stories and plays illustrating the more subtle aspects of the subject.
    $7.95

Everest-Aspiration

These inspired talks by one who has reached the pinnacle are the best and surest guideposts for others who also want to go upward to the highest, forward to the farthest and inward to the deepest.

Topics include: Dream and Reality • Satisfaction • Imagination • Intuition • Realisation $8.95

Siddhartha Becomes the Buddha

Who exactly was the Buddha? In these ten dramatic scenes, Sri Chinmoy answers this question from the deepest spiritual point of view. The combination of profound insight and simplicity of language makes this book an excellent choice for anyone, young or old, seeking to understand one of the world's most influential spiritual figures. $5.95

Peace-Blossom-Fragrance
Aphorisms on Peace

These 700 aphorisms offer a profound and illumining look at the divine nature of peace, it's relation to humanity's age-old quest, and secrets of its attainment and preservation. Special edition not available in stores. $7.95

My Flute

In this remarkable collection of poetry, Sri Chinmoy conveys the whole spectrum of spiritual emotions ranging from the doubts and fears of the wavering pilgrim to the ecstatic realisations of the illumined Master. In his role of the Seer-Poet, Sri Chinmoy writes with a power, lyricism and authenticity seldom encountered in this genre. $7.95

My Lord's Secrets Revealed

This book consists of a series of brief, revealing glimpses of God the Supreme Father by a spiritual Master who has experienced them firsthand. Many of the revelations take the form of conversations between Sri Chinmoy, the son, and his all-loving Father. These conversations convey the loving intimacy between God and man. $7.95

Songs of the Soul

This volume brings together Songs of the Soul and Blossoms of the Heart. Each work has a lyric emphasis of its own, though the theme of both is our relationship with God. Songs of the Soul are luminous expressions from the innermost being, voicing its identity with the eternal Truth. Their appeal is a direct call to our own inner light. Blossoms of the Heart speak to the upward-reaching aspiration in man, giving the seeker the assurance that his inner cry is never unheard. $7.95

MUSIC OF SRI CHINMOY

Flute Music for Meditation

While in a state of deep meditation Sri Chinmoy plays his haunting melodies on the electric echo-flute. Its rich and soothing tones will transport you to the highest realms of inner peace and harmony.   Cassette $9.95 CD $12.95

Inner and Outer Peace

A tapestry of music, poetry and aphorisms on inner and outer peace. Sri Chinmoy's profoundly inspiring messages are woven into a calm and uplifting musical composition with the Master singing, chanting and playing the flute, harmonium, esraj, cello, harpsichord and synthesizer.

Cassette $9.95

Ecstasy's Trance
Esraj Music for Meditation

The esraj, often described as a soothing combination of sitar and violin, is Sri Chinmoy's favourite instrument. With haunting intensity, he seems to draw the music from another dimension. The source of these compositions is the silent realm of the deepest and most sublime meditation. Listen to the music and enter this realm, a threshold rarely crossed in the course of one's lifetime.   Cassette $9.95

The Dance of Light
Sri Chinmoy Plays the Flute

Forty-seven soft and gentle flute melodies that will carry you directly to the source of joy and beauty: your own aspiring heart. Be prepared to float deep, deep within on waves of music that "come from Heaven itself."   Cassette $9.95

My Flute
Sri Chinmoy recites his poetry

In this remarkable collection of poetry, Sri Chinmoy conveys the whole spectrum of spiritual emotions ranging from the doubts and fears of the wavering pilgrim to the ecstatic realisations of the illumined Master. In his role of the Seer-Poet, Sri Chinmoy speaks with a power, lyricism and authenticity seldom encountered in this genre.

CD $9.95

To order books or tapes, request a catalogue, or find out more about Sri Chinmoy or the Sri Chinmoy Centres worldwide, please write to:

AUM PUBLICATIONS
86-10 Parsons Blvd.
Jamaica, NY 11432

When ordering a book or cassette, send check or money order made out to Aum Publications. Please add $3.50 postage for the first item and 50¢ for each additional item. Prices valid thru January 2000.